HOW HAS YOUR
PURPOSE
SHAPED YOUR
JOURNEY?

PERSONAL REFLECTIONS SECTION INCLUDED

SHASHAWNDA L. CARLTON

Scripture quotations marked NIV are taken from the Holy Bible, New International Version®, NIV®. Copyright © 1973, 1978, 1984, 2011 by Biblica, Inc.™ Used by permission of Zondervan. All rights reserved worldwide. www.zondervan.com

Scripture quotations marked KJV are from the King James version of the Bible.

Scripture marked NKJV taken from the New King James Version®. Copyright © 1982 by Thomas Nelson. Used by permission. All rights reserved.

Scripture quotations marked AMP are taken from the Amplified Bible, Copyright © 1954, 1958, 1962, 1964, 1965, 1987 by The Lockman Foundation. Used by permission.

Published by TJS Publishing House
www.tjspublishinghouse.com
IG: @ tjspublishinghouse
FB: @ tjspublishinghouse
tjspublishinghouse@gmail.com

Published in the United States of America

ISBN-13: 978-1-952833-17-5
ISBN-10: 1-952833-17-5

DEDICATION

I would like to dedicate this book to all single-parent families. Never stop pushing forward. Life will get better. The best is yet to come!

CONTENTS

ACKNOWLEDGMENTS

Without the strength of my family,
I would have never been able to share my story.
Termonja, thank you for being my Knight in shining armor.
Alex, Isaiah, and Joshua,
thank you for keeping Mommy focused.
Stay tuned to more from God's daughter.

INTRODUCTION

Are you ready to take a journey with me? Are you ready to revisit your past, so you can understand how it has shaped your future? Are you really ready?

Take this journey with me as I share pieces of my past and discuss how it has shaped my future. Since God has no respect for persons, he will do the same for you. Remember, there are a purpose and plan for you. Continue on your journey so you can see what the devil meant for evil works for your good.

As you read, stop and "tell" your story. As you read, stop and "reflect". As you read, "prepare" for the new you!

REMEMBER: *"I can do all things through Christ who strengthens me."*

Philippians 4:13 NKJV

1 ACCPETANCE

Serenity Prayer

*God, grant me the serenity to accept the things I cannot change,
courage to change the things I can,
and wisdom to know the difference.*

REINHOLD NIEBUHR

Why me? Have you ever asked yourself this question? Then have you heard someone say, "why not you"? Really? They do not know my problems or feel my pain. Here I was, a young, educated, active churchgoer, pregnant with no husband.

I blamed everyone! The father, my family, church members, co-workers, but not myself. Does that sound familiar? I felt, how could they? Why did this happen to me? How could I move forward? Again, why me?

As I began to slow down, take some deep breaths, and work on co-parenting plans with my child's father, I felt some pressure released. However, I was still pregnant and now moving from house to house. Also, barely keeping a job and sometimes homeless. Not only did I have to take care of myself, but now a baby as well.

Just as I felt the world was ending, there came God! After moving from place to place and sleeping on couches, a door opened. Just in time for my child!

My child arrived two months later. I could not believe it. I was about to become a mother. Was I ready? I better be as I did not have any other option but to move forward.

PHASE 2 OF LIFE

Personal Reflection:
What have you had to accept?

_____

_____

_____

_____

_____

_____

_____

_____

Personal Reflection Continued:
What have you had to accept?

_____

_____

_____

_____

_____

_____

_____

_____

2 STABILITY

"But the Lord is faithful, and he will strengthen you and protect you from the evil one."

2 Thessalonians 3:3 NIV

Now that my child is here, I have to step it up. I started attending church again. I moved from the back of the church back to the front. I was taking it one day at a time. I was finally able to obtain a car (a reliable one). I caught up on bills and was back to being focused at work. We even moved out of the housing projects and into a gated community. I started taking responsibility for my actions and putting my child first. I could finally see the light at the end of the tunnel.

Phase 3 of Life

Personal Reflection:
What does stability look like to you?

_____

_____

_____

_____

_____

_____

_____

_____

Personal Reflection Continued:

What does stability look like to you?

_____

_____

_____

_____

_____

_____

_____

_____

_____

3 DECISIONS

Decisions Are The Hardest Thing To Make, Especially When It Is A Choice Between Where You Should Be And Where You Want To Be.

Unknown

As I began to move forward, life started to happen. My child was getting older, and now I needed daycare. My job didn't seem to be enough, and we had to move again. Also, I had to get a second job, which meant another daycare was needed (as the first closed at 6 pm). Thank God my best friend's grandmother helped me by giving me a significantly discounted rate. Again, as I continued to focus on God and cry out to him for help, he reminded me to hold on.

One day while at work, I got a phone call. To my surprise, it was a high school classmate asking for a dinner date. I was not sure at first. I had not thought about a relationship (definitely not a serious one) after having a child. Was I attractive enough? Would he want a woman with a baby? What would everyone think? I mean, he was not my child's father.

Then I took a deep breath and said, "Girl, you could use a meal, and it's only a *dinner date, so why not?" To my surprise, we became close friends (almost like best friends) and started talking almost daily. I could tell him anything, and he was a good listener.*

Also, I could get my child into a more cost-efficient daycare and was thinking all was well. Then the trouble started again, but this time at work. My job was becoming rocky. There were many layoffs, and my manager and I were not on one accord. I felt there was always something going on. I mean, really?!

Phase 4 of Life

Personal Reflection:

What decisions have you had to make in life?

_____

_____

_____

_____

_____

_____

_____

_____

_____

Personal Reflection Continued:

What decisions have you had to make in life?

_____

_____

_____

_____

_____

_____

_____

_____

4 RESTORATION

So I will restore to you the

years that the

swarming locust

has eaten,

The crawling locust,

The consuming locust,

And the chewing locust,

My great army which I sent

among you.

Joel 2:25 NKJV

I had to believe God was up to something. I was starting to notice a trend. Every time life got rocky and unbearable, a blessing was coming, and I had to trust God even more. It made me think about faith and how it works. "Now faith is the substance of things hoped for, the evidence of things not seen." Hebrews 11:1 KJV

As time passed, I moved to a new city, and my friend became my husband. Then we had two children and became a blended family.

To date, I am a homeowner (no more moving), and my oldest child is in college. What a mighty God we serve!!

Current Phase of Life

Personal Reflection:

What has God restored in your life?

_____

_____

_____

_____

_____

_____

_____

_____

Personal Reflection Continued:
What has God restored in your life?

_____

_____

_____

_____

_____

_____

_____

_____

5 REFERENCES

- *Philippians 4:13 AMP*

- *Psalm 27:1-14 AMP*

- *Psalm 37: 1-40 AMP*

- *Psalm 25:1-22 AMP*

- *Psalm 91:1-16 AMP*

- *Psalm 46:1 AMP*

- *Psalm 23:1-6 AMP*

- *Hebrews 11:1 AMP*

List Your Resources

_____

_____

_____

_____

_____

_____

_____

_____

_____

ABOUT THE AUTHOR

ShaShawnda L. Carlton is a wife, mother, CEO of AIJ Connection Services Inc. (aijconnect.com), works as a program manager at a Fortune 500 Company, and now an author. She holds a master's degree in human resources and has extensive experience in group presentations, coaching, human resources, and she has earned several professional licenses and credentials to date.

During her free time, ShaShawnda likes to watch her children play sports and spend time with them and her husband.

Made in United States
Orlando, FL
27 November 2021

10839082R00022